Journal Four

Seasons of Hope

M. Donna MacLeod

Ave Maria Press AVE Notre Dame, Indiana

To Erynne Lee MacLeod,
a cherished daughter who loved Jesus
and now lives with him,
and
to her dad, my dear husband Bryan,
who has faithfully been by my side
every step of this life-giving ministry.

Founded in 1865, Ave Maria Press is a ministry of the United States Province of Holy Cross.

www.avemariapress.com

Paperback: ISBN-13 978-1-64680-236-4

E-book: ISBN-13 978-1-64680-280-7

Cover and text design by Katherine Robinson.

Printed and bound in the United States of America.

Contents

The Seasons of Hope Prayer can be easily found on the back cover of this book.

Welcome to
Seasons of Hope Journal Four

Dear Brothers and Sisters in Christ Jesus,

When your loved one went home to the Lord, did you think that God was calling you to a new life in him, too? And that this new life held much more than pain and sorrow?

I had no idea what lay ahead when my daughter Erynne died. Years of caring for the dying and their families as a nurse did not prepare me for my own grief. Yet God would use the lessons I learned for the good of others. From the loss of a precious child, a Christ-centered ministry to the bereaved and a hospice were born. God plans ahead. He didn't forget me, my family, or my community, and he hasn't forgotten you. He wants to console you.

Trusting in God and opening your mind and soul to the Seasons of Hope program blesses you in untold ways. Your broken heart will start to mend as your spirit lifts. I've seen it happen time and again.

Perhaps this *Journal* reached you through the kindness of a concerned friend who knew its mini-retreats with Jesus could ease your sorrow. Or maybe you found all four of the program journals on your own and plan to use them each day or once a week until the sessions are finished. Or you may have wanted to attend a Seasons of Hope group at church but couldn't, so someone from the ministry team sent you a *Journal* and possibly offered to call you each week to support your efforts.

Most likely, though, you have this *Journal* because you joined a Seasons of Hope group that meets at church or online. You might be attending for the first time. Or you might have a season or two under your belt and are back for more. You realize that the support of others who know what you are going through will once more bless your grief journey with God's gift of love.

Whether you use the *Journals* independently or have group support, you are a vital part of this powerful ministry. Grounded in scripture and the healing wisdom, traditions, and practices of the Catholic Church, Seasons of Hope truly focuses on faith and the spiritual side of grieving. In the midst of suffering, it can draw you ever closer to the Lord. What a gift from heaven that is!

A *Journal* and a Bible are all you need for group sessions or independent journaling. You begin each week with the Seasons of Hope Prayer, located on the back cover of this *Journal*. Then you turn to a new Guidepost page for the title, theme, and scripture citation to locate the Bible passage that guides the session. On the next page you will find the Marking the Route activity that draws from the scripture's theme. The adjoining Notes page has space to write your thoughts related to the exercise.

If you attend a group, the facilitator will have faith-sharing questions based on the session's scripture story for you and the other participants to consider. And you also enrich your weekly journey with the *Journal*'s retreat-like Soul Work that you do at home after the session.

If you are a journaler, you read the session's Bible story and do the Marking the Route exercises plus soothe the wounds of your heart and soul with the Soul Work. The process generally takes about twenty minutes, a commitment that most schedules can handle.

The Soul Work's theme and opening comments in Looking Back offer a fresh way to view the scripture story. You then ask for guidance in A Prayer to Find the Way. You will read Steps along the Path to learn how the scripture story relates to mourning and then spend time with the Reflection section to consider your situation. You can write your thoughts in the space provided under the heading Journal Entry.

To help you cope, Moving Forward offers a Church tradition or act of charity that generates hope. You finish the Soul Work with the Closing Prayer to thank God for the gift of consolation.

The appendix at the end of the booklet has some treasures of its own. Are you interested in literature and websites about losing a loved one? Check out Helpful Resources, which also includes links to sacred images used for contemplation in some sessions. Are you in a group? Use the Network Directory to record contact information about your new friends in Christ. How about ground rules for the group? That's covered in the Guide to Group Etiquette. Want to help your facilitators plan for the next season? The Season Survey lets you formally share your ideas.

By using this *Seasons of Hope Journal Four*, you bring the trials of your loss to the Lord. You embrace his teachings, reflect on your loss, and share the painful moments so that your wounded spirit can grow strong in him.

May Seasons of Hope's unique way of placing Jesus Christ at the center of your grief bring you consolation and healing.

In Christ our Hope,
M. Donna MacLeod

Session 1

Guidepost: Point of Departure

Theme: Last Encounter

Scripture: John 14:1–8

Marking the Route

Exercise:
Questions about eternal life occupy all of us—sometimes quite intensely, as when a loved one dies. Our views about what happens to the soul when someone dies start forming when we are children. To take a look at what your parents and other family members taught you about life after death and their way of grieving, complete these statements:

- My name is ______________________________.

- Things my parents/family believed about life after death include . . .

- When someone we loved died, my parents/family taught me that God . . .

- To ease their own grief, my parents/family would . . .

- Back then, when I was sad over losing someone dear, I would . . .

Notes

Soul Work: Point of Departure

Looking Back: *The Father's House*

In this week's passage from John 14:1–8, the feast of the Passover is underway in Jerusalem. Jesus and his closest disciples are gathered in the city. Well aware that religious officials want to arrest him, Jesus knows he will soon leave his disciples to return to the Father.

To console the men, Jesus reminds them of their faith in God the Father. The father figure played a tremendous role in the culture and law of the Hebrew people. As ruler of the household, a father was responsible for all family members. The fatherhood of God and his covenant with them would ensure their place in the Father's house.

Thomas admits the fear the group has: they cannot follow Jesus home. They aren't sure where he is going. Jesus explains that if they know him, they know the way to the Father.

The Hebrew word for "to know" involves more than grasping something intellectually. It suggests an activity of the heart and mind, a familiarity through experience. To know God, you must open yourself to the divine will, acknowledge God as your source, and worship with gratitude. You know God when you keep the divine commandments out of love.

Like so many of us, the apostles cannot fathom life after death. Jesus speaks of many dwelling places in the Father's house, where they will live forever. He will prepare a place for them. In fact, he promises to come back to bring them to heaven. We now know that Jesus's death and Resurrection opened the house of the Father to all who believe in him.

A Prayer to Find the Way

O Lord,
like your apostles,
I find it hard to imagine
what life after death truly holds,
but I believe
that my departed loved one
lives with you.
I am left behind,
but the path of mourning
is brighter because of you.
Amen.

Steps along the Path

The truth about the heavenly kingdom of God stirs up confusion even today. Church scholars through the ages have offered the idea of heaven (the abode of God, angels, saints, and the faithful departed) as a celestial paradise and place of eternal happiness. What is lost on some is that the bliss of heaven flows from blessed unity with God that begins in this life and is perfected in the next.

When you lose someone dear, being left behind can be overwhelming. You might have moments when you forget that the person is gone and call out his or her name. Grief can also injure spiritual bonds and leave you feeling abandoned by God.

Jesus and his apostles were together for quite a while. Much like you and your loved one, they wanted more time with each other even in life after death. Jesus doesn't want you to be troubled. He promised to come to his friends. How is your friendship with him going these days?

Reflection

Jesus spoke of preparing a dwelling place in the Father's house for his friends. Imagine Jesus actually getting some heavenly place ready. What might he do to make your loved one feel at home?

Journal Entry

When your loved one went home to the Lord, your life changed. Write to the Lord about how it feels to be left behind. Tell him how grieving affects your prayer life.

Moving Forward

If traditional prayers have become difficult for you to say during mourning, you may want to try something called "centering prayer." It is simple to do. Find a peaceful place and take a few deep breaths to clear your mind. Then focus on the person of Jesus by repeating his name in the silence of your heart. Listen to the silence and become aware of the Lord's presence.

Closing Prayer

O loving Savior,
with a grateful heart
I remember my loved one.
I pray that, if it be your will,

____

will dwell with you and the Father
in heaven.
I pray in your name.
Amen.

Session 2

Guidepost: Path to Understanding

Theme: The Garden of Gethsemane

Scripture: Mark 14:32–42

Marking the Route

Exercise:
The remarkable scene in the Garden of Gethsemane reveals Jesus's way of coping. He prayed fervently to the Father as he struggled with what was to come, yet he desired above all else to fulfill the Father's will.

Imagine being in a garden where you feel close to God. Consider the things that the Father could help you with in your time of distress. Make a list of those requests in the space below.

Notes

Soul Work: Path to Understanding

Looking Back: *Betrayal*

The story in Mark 14:32–42 is often referred to as the Agony in the Garden. We can only imagine what Peter, James, and John witnessed at Gethsemane, but the account tells us that Jesus wants them nearby as he prays. Before praying, however, Jesus grows troubled and distressed. The nature of his anguish becomes clear when he says that his "soul" is sorrowful even to death. This spiritual struggle deepens as the fateful act of betrayal draws near.

Jesus foresees what is coming, but his companions are clueless. In their own way, they contribute to the Lord's distress by failing to keep watch. Betrayed by his own and those who oppose his mission, Jesus prays and surrenders his human will to the divine will of the Father, a commendable example for sorrowful souls of the ages.

A Prayer to Find the Way

O generous Jesus,
you took on the sins of humanity
out of divine love for us.
My soul is filled with sorrow,
yet in you I find courage.
Help me when betrayal visits
my time of mourning.
Amen.

Steps along the Path

If you have sat through the night at the bedside of an ill loved one, you probably can relate to the apostles who failed to keep their eyes open for the Lord. As with Peter, James, and John, the spirit may be willing, but the body is weak. Surely the apostles had good intentions when they agreed to accompany the Lord and perhaps lift him up in prayer.

Judas Iscariot, the betrayer Jesus alluded to, has intrigued scholars for centuries. Some question whether Judas forced a crisis to make Jesus perform an unmistakable sign to prove he was the Messiah. If that was Judas's purpose, he proved that good intentions aren't always what they seem.

Sometimes friends or family members think they are helpful when, in fact, their behavior is hurtful. It could be an insensitive comment, keeping their distance, or not carrying out the wishes of a loved one. Whether the failure is on a small scale like that of Peter, James, and John or larger like that of Judas, chances are you will at some point feel betrayed on your journey of mourning.

Reflection

During grieving, it's normal to grapple with your own past behavior that might have been unsupportive. Would you do anything differently if your loved one were alive today?

Also dwell on the good intentions you acted on that met with success.

Journal Entry

Even in a healthy relationship, miscommunication can pose a problem. Both parties may be able to forgive, but often the subconscious stores the unpleasant memory.

Write to Jesus and seek his healing touch for a hurtful memory involving you and your loved one. If none exists, give glory and thanks to God in writing.

Moving Forward

The posture we assume during prayer speaks volumes. Jesus and his followers probably prayed standing. This noble stance reflects the belief that we are made in God's likeness. In Mark's account, Jesus fell to the ground when he solemnly prayed to his Father in the Garden of Gethsemane (Lk 22:41). Whether he was prostrate or kneeling, Jesus's posture conveys complete dependence on God the Father.

As a sign of respect, we stand during the reading of the gospel and at other moments of prayer during the liturgy. We kneel during the consecration to reverence Christ present in the Eucharist, to express penitence and sorrow for sins, and to offer private prayers of petition and thanks to God.

We genuflect (bend a knee) before the tabernacle, which houses the Blessed Sacrament. We bow or genuflect before the altar, the consecrated site of the holy sacrifice of the Mass.

Each time you genuflect or bow at church this week, think of the sorrow in the Lord's heart as he fell to the ground in the Garden of Gethsemane.

Closing Prayer

Lord Jesus Christ,
your obedience to the Father's will
brought salvation to humanity.
I give you thanks
and humbly offer my sorrow to you,
trusting in your infinite love
and tender mercy.
Amen.

Session 3

Guidepost: Obstacles on the Journey

Theme: Crown of Thorns

Scripture: John 19:1–3

Marking the Route

Exercise:
It is hard to fathom the cruelty and physical pain Jesus experienced at the hands of his enemies. But a symbol of the Passion such as the crown of thorns can help us imagine the Lord's suffering of mind, body, and soul. Grieving may not brutalize the body, but it does impact both our physical and mental health. Grieving also affects the health of our soul. Spiritually speaking, our suffering unites us more closely to Jesus. From that closeness comes the knowledge of who Jesus truly is.

Contemplate the crown of thorns image that's on display, on a prayer card, or available at the Stations of the Cross link in the appendix. Or simply consider a rose with prickly thorns to launch your thoughts. Reflect on Jesus's suffering and yours.

Then write to Jesus about how you deal with the emotional and spiritual pain of your grief.

Notes

Soul Work: Obstacles on the Journey

Looking Back: *Suffering*

The passage of John 19:1–3 recollects what happened during Jesus's trial before Pilate. The crowds had demanded that Barabbas, not Jesus, be set free. Pilate was not convinced Jesus was guilty of a crime. To appease the crowd, Pilate sent him to be flogged.

Flogging, a severe punishment that often led to death in Jesus's day, was reserved for disobedient slaves or noncitizens of Rome. The criminal had to lie at the feet of a soldier and receive lashes to his bare chest and back with leather straps or chains studded with bones, metal, or spikes.

History indicates that Jesus was handed over for the cruelest of beatings. When blows that break bone, whips that sting, and thorns that stab through flesh were not enough to break Jesus's spirit, the soldiers resorted to mockery. Jesus endured all this before the heavy cross was laid upon his shoulders.

Jesus surely knew suffering. Can you imagine the sorrow in his divine heart as he faced his destiny at the hands of cruelty?

A Prayer to Find the Way

O Savior of my soul,
you endured suffering
that is beyond my comprehension.
In your suffering,
was your heart breaking?
My heart aches for you now,
though I know you gave your life freely.
Help me keep you in mind
as I face grief and its trials.
Amen.

Steps along the Path

The soldiers who tortured Jesus put a crown of thorns and a cloak of purple (the color of royalty) on him to mock him and draw jeers from the hostile crowd. When you consider that purple also denotes spirituality, the fake king's cloak evokes the spiritual suffering endured by Jesus, the King of Kings.

When you lose a loved one, your spirit may be troubled with its own form of suffering. Do you carry something of that person with you to lift your spirits? A memento can help you remember the good times and lessen your fear of losing those memories. It can be something to lean on, helping you down the path of spiritual healing and growth.

Reflection

In the midst of grieving, it's hard to imagine you can get through the pain. Sorrow takes its toll and drains the energy needed for healing. Think about the resurrected Jesus. How does he appear to you? Are his wounds healed?

Journal Entry

How far have you come in healing after losing your loved one? Have you considered your progress? Writing down your thoughts helps put your experience into perspective. Just let the words flow out of you. You may be surprised at what you learn.

Moving Forward

The scripture this week reveals the brutality that Jesus suffered when he shed his blood at Calvary. During the consecration at Mass, ordinary wine made from grapes becomes for us the Blood of Christ and ordinary bread becomes for us the Body of Christ.

Next time you receive the chalice, think of the blood Jesus shed for all humanity. If the cup is not offered, remember the Lord's suffering as the priest prays the words of consecration.

Closing Prayer

O risen Lord,
through the shedding
of your Precious Blood
salvation came.
I am eternally grateful
for all that you do for me.
Let my grieving bring good to others.
Amen.

Session 4

Guidepost: Path to Inner Healing

Theme: Gift of Caring

Scripture: John 19:25–30

Marking the Route

Exercise:
You know who your friends are when misfortune befalls you. At the end of Jesus's journey, only the youngest apostle, John, joined Mary and the faithful women disciples who stood at the foot of the Cross.

Write a letter to Jesus. Let him know who has stood by you in your time of sorrow. Express your gratitude for the gift of their concern and their acts of kindness. If no one comes to mind, write about the gift of Seasons of Hope.

Notes

Soul Work: Path to Inner Healing

Looking Back: *Infinite Thirst*

If you read John 19:25–30 literally, it seems that Jesus is simply stating that he is thirsty. After all, he was hung on a cross to die. His parched mouth and throat signal dehydration from loss of blood, lack of adequate fluids to drink, and the heat. He would be thirsty.

The gospel writer, however, says Jesus's complaint of thirst fulfills scripture, referring perhaps to Psalms 22 and 69 as possible sources of what was uttered. Both psalms lament the plight of the righteous sufferer who trusts God to rescue him.

Since Jesus is within minutes of dying, some feel that his "thirst" holds even greater significance for humanity. The message is so simple that it can easily be overlooked. Jesus thirsts for our love. He loves us and wants us to love him. Throughout his life, his mission existed because of this eternal love. His ardent desire and yearning for our love are tremendous gifts that bring new life to the weary.

Here's a question to ask yourself: how does losing a loved one affect your love of Jesus?

A Prayer to Find the Way

O Jesus, my redeemer,
may your thirst for my love
be quenched through my devotion
to you.
Let my sorrow find consolation in you
on the way
to spiritual healing.
Amen.

Steps along the Path

Is there any time more troubled in life than when a painful death is upon someone? Hanging from a cross as though he were a criminal, Jesus was in excruciating pain. His swollen, bleeding body required fluids. When Jesus expressed his need, someone took pity and offered a sponge soaked with wine.

That act of kindness showed compassion, the essence of the Savior himself. Even during suffering, Jesus brought out the best in others. Has suffering through your sorrow brought out the best in you?

Reflection

Jesus accomplished the greatest act of love—he gave up his life for the salvation of all who believe in him. During mourning, you may not feel lovable, but you are. Jesus chose you, and the depth of his love surpasses all understanding. Think about his love for you.

Journal Entry

Even relationships made in heaven don't always run smoothly. Losing a loved one can leave the most devout person with plenty of questions for the Lord. Write to Jesus about your grief and honestly share what is on your mind.

Moving Forward

In Jesus's final moments, he was the consummate minister of consolation. He wanted his mother Mary and his friend John to console each other. Scripture tells us they honored his plan.

This week follow the lead of Mary and John by reaching out to someone who also has lost a loved one. Share your concern with a visit, a phone call, a card, a letter, an email, or a text message. Not only will an act of kindness make the recipient feel better, but you will feel better, too. Just try it.

Closing Prayer

O Jesus, consoler of us all,
thank you from the bottom
of my heart
for the promise of eternal life.
Your love for me is infinitely more
than I deserve.
Let my life reflect my love for you.
Amen.

Session 5

Guidepost: Way of Suffering

Theme: Why Have You Forsaken Me?

Scripture: Mark 15:22–34

Marking the Route

Exercise:
When a loved one dies, we can feel forsaken by the unfairness of life, medical personnel, the deceased, onlookers, and even God. In a sense, something within us has died. It's called trust.

Let the image of Divine Mercy on display, on a prayer card, or posted online guide you through this exercise. Notice Jesus's expression, posture, gestures, the symbols of holiness, and the rays of his merciful fountain of grace. What catches your eye? Think about the message, "Jesus, I trust in You." Let Jesus speak to your heart. Then share your thoughts in writing with him.

Note: Next session, have an item with you that shows your love for your dearly departed one.

Notes

Soul Work: Way of Suffering

Looking Back: *Hurtful Words*

The Crucifixion passage of Mark 15:22–34 brings us to Golgotha ("skull place"), a little hill located northwest of Jerusalem where condemned criminals were executed. To deliver the Lord to this unholy place was a cruel gesture in itself, symbolic of the humiliation intended by those who had found him guilty of religious and political crimes.

If Jesus wanted to withdraw from the horror of the Crucifixion, he could have drunk the wine laced with myrrh that would act like a narcotic to ease his pain and awareness. Yet he refuses the drink, showing his total acceptance of God's will. The merciless ridicule he receives at the hands of his enemies surely intensifies the torture of being nailed to the Cross.

The sign placed on the Cross that reads "The King of the Jews" is not meant as a sign of honor and respect. As was customary, it states the crime of the one being crucified. It makes Jesus a target of contempt, inciting soldiers and passersby to scoff at him. We can only try to imagine how their insults must have pierced the tender, loving heart of our Savior.

Nearby, the chief priests and scribes smugly gossip about Jesus, demanding that he come down from the Cross. If you have ever been verbally kicked when you're down, you know how hurtful malicious words can be. The derogatory comments from the criminal beside Jesus surely add to his agony.

A Prayer to Find the Way

O loving Lord,
you suffered so much for us.
Give me the wisdom
to forgive those who hurt me.
I ask that kindness be the root
of all that I do.
Amen.

Steps along the Path

Unkind words wield a sometimes surprisingly destructive power and often inflict great pain. The sting of comments you might encounter during grieving often comes from well-intentioned people, but callousness takes a toll nonetheless.

Insensitive remarks happen so commonly during bereavement that much is written about what to say and what not to say to the grieving. In fact, a huge concern of people of compassion is that they might say something offensive to a mourner. Fear keeps some from reaching out or from making a phone call or a visit that is sorely needed by both parties. Which side of the dilemma have you encountered?

Reflection

Dealing with injured feelings takes energy, particularly when you grieve. Does something come to mind that hurt your feelings since your loss? Did you say something you wish you hadn't said? Now consider the circumstances. What do you think Jesus would advise you to do with your feelings?

Journal Entry

Hurtful remarks can slay the spirit. It only makes sense to bring your wounds to Jesus, the healer of the soul. Write to him about the situation you just reflected on and listen for his wisdom in your heart.

Moving Forward

Suffering offers a chance to grow spiritually, although it rarely seems like a gift from God when you're in its throes. Mourning a loved one is a form of suffering that wounds the spirit.

Like Jesus on the Cross, you too can call out to God for help and expect to receive it. When you are ready, let the Holy Spirit lead you beyond asking for assistance with your sorrow. Try giving God praise because he is God, the eternal source of love.

Closing Prayer

O triune God,
fountain of wisdom
and all consolation,
you alone know how
to heal my wounded heart and soul.
All glory and praise to you forever!
Amen.

Session 6

Guidepost: Final Destination

Theme: Be My Witnesses

Scripture: Acts 1:6–11

Marking the Route

Exercise (for a group member):
Show the group something that reminds you of the love you shared with your departed loved one and tell why it's special to you.

Exercise (for a journaler):
At each session, you have honored your deceased loved one with word and prayer. Today, go a step further. Consider the item you selected for this session that reminds you of the love you shared with your departed loved one. Write about why it is special to you.

Note: Seasons of Hope *has four different seasons. Find out when the next one starts.*

Notes

Soul Work: Final Destination

Looking Back: *Patience*

The disciples want to know God's timetable, but this week's scripture reading (Acts 1:6–11) makes it clear that Jesus is not about to discuss the Father's plan. The disciples have to wait in hope for God's will to be done. Waiting will teach them many lessons about patience.

Jesus is the model of patience. The disciples' question to him about restoring the kingdom to Israel must have given him pause. How many times had he explained his mission to them? He came to reveal the Father's love, yet they cling to the ancient notion that the Messiah would be a political leader—someone to reestablish Israel's independence.

Instead of scolding them, Jesus promises the gift of the Holy Spirit to empower them to do God's work. The work is far from politics. By the power of the Holy Spirit, they will have faith in God; bring healing of body, mind, heart, soul, will, intellect, and emotion to God's people; and perform miracles of all kinds—a remarkable reward for people who had a hard time grasping the mission of the Messiah.

A Prayer to Find the Way

O patient Savior,
I am like the disciples
who misunderstood your plans.
They wished for something
meant for another time.
Help me accept
the trials of mourning
with trust in you.
Amen.

Steps along the Path

If you are willing to bear trials calmly and without complaint, you are a patient person. God molded you that way, so consider yourself blessed. What an inspiration you are for those around you!

Yet patience with oneself during mourning can be a challenge for many of us. We might accept the trials of grieving, but we usually expect them to pass more quickly. We grow impatient as time goes on, which may suggest we have room for spiritual growth.

Mourning seems like an unlikely time to learn how to be more patient, doesn't it? But what if God wants to use our grief to help us grow closer to him?

This week's scripture sheds light on the dilemma. Jesus recognized the grief and impatience of his disciples. So what did he do? He promised to send them the Holy Spirit. They would receive the power and patience (a fruit of the Holy Spirit) to overcome their grief and carry on his mission.

How can you grow in patience? Ask Jesus to send you what you need.

Reflection

How patient are you when life is going smoothly? Are you more patient with others lately? Or has your level of tolerance for everyday inconveniences lessened? Does losing a loved one make you wonder if the heartache will ever end?

Journal Entry

With the Reflection questions in mind, write to Jesus about what you hope for these days.

Moving Forward

The Resurrection of Jesus gave the disciples new hope in him. We can only imagine their thoughts as the Lord ascended into heaven, but we know they took that hope and went forth to be his witnesses to the ends of the earth. You too hope in Jesus and are called to go forth with the life you have been given.

Focus on the resurrected Lord by praying the Glorious Mysteries of the Rosary. Let his ever-patient mother be your guide. For more information on praying the Rosary, check out the Helpful Resources section in the appendix.

Closing Prayer

O God of patience and kindness,
thank you for the unique being
you made me
and for your generous gifts
of the Spirit.
With a grateful heart,
I wait for resurrection
from the depths of my sorrow.
Amen.

Appendix

Helpful Resources

Books

DeLorenzo, Leonard J. *Our Faithful Departed: Where They Are and Why It Matters.* Notre Dame, IN: Ave Maria Press, 2022.

Gilbert, Richard B. *Finding Your Way after Your Parent Dies: Hope for Grieving Adults.* Notre Dame, IN: Ave Maria Press, 1999.

Helping Children Cope with Death. Portland: Dougy Center, 2015.

Helping Teens Cope with Death. Portland: Dougy Center, 2015.

Hickman, Martha Whitmore. *Healing after Loss: Daily Meditations for Working through Grief.* New York: Avon Books, 1994.

Kübler-Ross, Elisabeth, and David Kessler. *On Grief and Grieving: Finding the Meaning of Grief through the Five Stages of Loss.* New York: Scribner, 2005.

Lafser, Christine O'Keeffe. *An Empty Cradle, a Full Heart: Reflections for Mothers and Fathers after Miscarriage, Stillbirth, or Infant Death.* Chicago: Loyola Press, 1998.

Noel, Brook, and Pamela D. Blair. *I Wasn't Ready to Say Goodbye: Surviving, Coping, and Healing after the Sudden Death of a Loved One.* Naperville, IL: Sourcebooks, 2008.

Nouwen, Henri J. M. *Turn My Mourning into Dancing: Finding Hope in Hard Times.* Nashville: Thomas Nelson, 2001.

O'Connor, Mary-Frances. *The Grieving Brain: The Surprising Science of How We Learn from Love and Loss.* New York: Harper One, 2022.

O'Hearn, Patrick, Bryan Feger, Kelly and Ryan Breaux. *The Grief of Dads: Support and Hope for Catholic Fathers Navigating Child Loss.* Notre Dame, IN: Ave Maria Press, 2023.

Roe, Gary. *Comfort for the Grieving Parent's Heart: Hope and Healing After Losing Your Child.* Cleveland: Healing Resources, 2020.

Rowland, Joanna. *The Memory Box: A Book about Grief. Illustrations by Thea Baker.* Minneapolis: Sparkhouse Family, 2017.

Rupp, Joyce. *Now That You've Gone Home: Courage and Comfort for Times of Grief.* Notre Dame, IN: Ave Maria Press, 2009.

Shoener, Ed, and John P. Dolan, eds. *When a Loved One Dies by Suicide: Comfort, Hope, and Healing for Grieving Catholics.* Notre Dame, IN: Ave Maria Press, 2020.

Tighe, Tommy. *St. Dymphna's Playbook: A Catholic Guide to Finding Mental and Emotional Well-Being.* Notre Dame, IN: Ave Maria Press, 2021.

White, Michael, and Tom Corcoran. *Seriously, God? Making Sense of Life Not Making Sense.* Notre Dame, IN: Ave Maria Press, 2021.

Wolfelt, Alan. *Understanding Your Grief: Ten Essential Touchstones for Finding Hope and Healing Your Heart.* Fort Collins, CO: Companion Press, 2021.

Zonnebelt-Smeege, Susan J., and Robert C. De Vries. *Getting to the Other Side of Grief: Overcoming the Loss of a Spouse.* Grand Rapids, MI: Baker Books, 2019.

Websites

www.bible.usccb.org/bible provides free access to the New American Bible.

www.hospicefoundation.org has a treasure trove of articles on grief and grieving.

www.whatsyourgrief.com offers grief and bereavement education and social media resources for adults, teens, and children.

www.widowedparent.org supports widowed mothers and fathers with children in the home.

www.avemariapress.com has books on prayer, bereavement, and spiritual enrichment.

www.compassionatefriends.org offers information and support for families who lose a child.

www.grasphelp.org supports those who have lost a loved one through the misuse of drugs.

www.healgrief.org provides grief resources, virtual groups, educational programs, and a map to find local and national support.

www.samaritanshope.org links to information on suicide-survivor issues for all ages.

www.taps.org helps those grieving the death of a military loved one by providing free grief resources, including casework, counseling, publications, retreats, seminars, and more.

Sacred Images

"Divine Mercy," www.thedivinemercy.org/message.

"Rosary," https://rosarycenter.org/how-to-pray-the-rosary.

"Sacred Heart of Jesus," https://m.theholyrosary.org/sacredheart/.

"Stations of the Cross," https://aleteia.org/2018/03/30/pray-the-stations-of-the-cross-with-these-beautiful-images-and-prayers/.

Network Directory

Interacting with others of faith who understand what it means to lose a loved one gives you a chance to give and receive support. Use the space below for contact information of participants in your Seasons of Hope group.

Name____

Phone number__________________________________

Email____

Name____

Phone number__________________________________

Email____

Name____

Phone number__________________________________

Email____

Name____

Phone number__________________________________

Email____

Name____

Phone number________________________________

Email_______________________________________

Name____

Phone number________________________________

Email_______________________________________

Name____

Phone number________________________________

Email_______________________________________

Name____

Phone number________________________________

Email_______________________________________

Name____

Phone number________________________________

Email_______________________________________

Guide to Group Etiquette

A facilitator guides the faith-sharing process by keeping the focus on the Lord and the session questions. A facilitator doesn't teach, preach, or advise. The facilitator creates a safe place for you to talk about your feelings about loss and receive consolation.

You are expected to

- come each week and make it known if you can't;
- arrive on time;
- treat others with respect;
- share your faith story and then let others talk;
- be a good listener;
- keep what is shared in confidence; and
- be open to God touching you through others.

Don't worry if tears flow. They are part of grieving. Smiles and laughter are welcome, too.

Season Survey

Please take a few moments to complete the statements below about your experience with our Seasons of Hope group. Thank you!

1. I learned about Seasons of Hope from

2. I think the meeting room is

3. For me, the session time is

4. For me, the length of the weekly sessions is

5. The focus on prayer, scripture, and God is

6. Private time to write, listen to music, or read allows me to

7. I find faith sharing

8. For me, the fellowship break is

9. Soul Work between sessions lets me

10. What I learned from Seasons of Hope is

11. When the next Seasons of Hope group forms, I

12. I'd also like to say

Date: ______________________________

Name (optional): ______________________________

Acknowledgments

How grateful I am to God for the blessing of so many who made this updated edition of the *Seasons of Hope Leader's Guide* and *Journals* possible. Only God can make goodness flow from the sorrow we bear. And I truly believe the Seasons of Hope program embodied in these books is a powerful witness to that reality.

My heartfelt thanks remain with the clergy, family, friends, and bereaved who believed long ago that this work would enrich our parishes. They were right! I'm also grateful to everyone who lifts us up in prayer and to the brokenhearted who trust in the Lord and come to be comforted. I appreciate the priests, deacons, religious sisters and brothers, lay pastoral advisors, and diocesan leaders that welcome the program. And I admire the amazing Seasons of Hope facilitators and helpers, at my side and everywhere else, who have faithfully poured their gifts, talents, and compassion into season after season of this Catholic grief-support ministry. Their feedback is woven into this edition.

The ongoing enthusiasm and expertise of the Ave Maria Press professionals and staff are greatly appreciated. Many thanks especially to Eileen Ponder, Karey Circosta, Erin Pierce, and Stephanie Sibal for championing this new edition.

As always, my husband Bryan's wisdom, love, faith, and generous spirit greatly influenced this work. I treasure the input of our dear daughter Meganne, who remains a constant source of love and support, and the memory of our dear Erynne, whose death opened my heart to all who mourn.

M. Donna MacLeod is a Catholic leader and founder of the Seasons of Hope ministry to the bereaved. She is the author of the program's bestselling *Leader's Guide* and four companion journals. This work was inspired by the loss of her youngest daughter, Erynne, in 1988 and the compassionate response of her parish.

MacLeod holds bachelor's and master's degrees in nursing and has served as an oncology clinical specialist, nurse educator, administrator, and hospice professional. She served on the board of trustees and training faculty of the former National Catholic Ministry to the Bereaved and is a member of the Catholic Family Life Association.

Macleod delivers keynotes, workshops, retreats, and other presentations online and at numerous national and diocesan conferences and parish events related to grief, loss, and ministry leadership in the United States and Canada. A seasoned ministry mentor, MacLeod supports Seasons of Hope facilitators with online resources and an enrichment series sponsored by Ave Maria Press. She also leads parish Seasons of Hope groups in the Diocese of Fall River, Massachusetts

She lives with her husband, Bryan, in the Boston, Massachusetts, area. She can be reached at seasonsofhope35@gmail.com.